The Memoirs of Angela

A High Price for a Low Life

Angela Sampson- Jarrett

ISBN: 978-1-956247-01-5

Dedication

I dedicate this book to Kevin, my wonderful, amazing husband. You have been my backbone through all of this. You listened when I became frustrated and helped me to push through—nursing me through this with love and affection. Thank you, and I love you. Kalinda, Nicole, Lakiah, Shardai, Eiontai, and Carlos, mommy loves you all very much…

Acknowledgement

I want to first thank God for giving me the strength, the wisdom, and the courage to write this book. I want to thank my family for being there when I needed an encouraging word. I want to thank my husband, Kevin Jarrett, for being my biggest supporter, never giving up on me. I love you, babe. I want to thank my granny, Gladys Wise, for loving me enough to take care of me when I needed you.

CONTENTS

About the Author

Angela Sampson- Jarrett is a wife, a mother of three wonderful children and a grandmother of three of the most angelic beauties. Angela went through struggles of substance abuse to change her life to a productive member of society.

Angela is a Licensed Independent Chemical Dependency Counselor. She has a Master's in Social Work and a Master's in Addiction Counseling. She is currently working on her Doctoral Degree in Psychology at Grand Canyon University. Angela owns and operates a Treatment Facility for Men who suffer from the disease of addiction. Angela's ultimate goal is to give back what is so freely given.

Preface

Drugs and alcohol are considered the elixir of life. How paradoxical it is that they are also the essence of death. Those who have not drunk do not know the simple pleasures of life. But those who do know that all pleasure is derived from it. A high price for a low life. In the beginning, the reasons for indulgence are very apparent. Unresolved issues, childhood trauma, heartbreak, the loss of a loved one, or parental neglect—any one of these reasons could lead to a dependency on the poison of your choice. However, as time passes, those reasons fade into the background and become unintelligible.

If an individual was to ask me why I got into substance abuse, I might not be able to give them one good answer. But the truth of the matter is, there is a void that needs to be filled, no matter what. Hence, an individual is likely to fall into the pothole of drug addiction. If seen from what scholars have defined the poison one chooses for himself, it is the use of a drug that is viewed as posing a problem by a society concerned. Drug addiction can be counted as a disease that does not discriminate and can impact anyone—regardless of age, gender, ethnicity, body type, or personal beliefs. Alcoholism and drug addiction may be the end product of various other factors, too, like biological, psychological, social, and environmental.

Drug addiction and sobriety are two sides of the same coin. Being sober at a place and then wholly violent just with the addictive poison is what the actual game is about. Some people might encounter diving into alcohol at an early age, mainly due to the stress, traumas, sexual assault, or violence they have been subjected to. Kids are just like monkeys; seeing their surroundings, one can quickly adapt to their life patterns, hence drinking or doing drugs. Exploring different avenues regarding drugs at a young age can prompt issues sometime down the road, particularly in your 20s and 30s. This is particularly evident when young people participate in regular hard-core boozing. Growing up around family members and close relatives who suffer from alcoholism or drug addiction increases the risk of alcohol or drug abuse for generations to come.

Indulgence in drugs has a way back. It is critical to recognize that even if a person can improve their alertness and awareness, they must still not drive or make important decisions until the drug is ultimately out of their system. This book tells and elaborates that drug addiction is recoverable. Since the brain holds the ropes of our actions and mind games, nothing is impossible if you believe in yourself, even leaving drugs. The trouble is that quitting is rarely easy, and the best solution isn't always clear. In this book, you will find how I got addicted to drugs and how you should believe that getting rid of this abuse is not impossible. It's all in your head. But what may seem like it is in your head may also take over your entire body, your entire being.

My life has taught me a lot, but it was not the kindest of teachers. It was hardly a teacher. I only observed my life and learned what I had to. Substance abuse has been a very consistent part of my initial existence. But it does not define me, nor will it ever. This book has written in it the depths of my chaotic but sequentially orderly life. Having a Master's in addiction Counseling, I only want to humanize the addictive aspect of existence.

Despite my difficult existence, I have learned enough to prevent others from falling into the same trap. I have learned enough to laugh about it now and then, even. Because what good is a life that is not even mildly amusing? I thank God for everything and for giving me the strength and resolve to be who I am and learn what I know.

Chapter 1

Possum Point

Having the attention span of your run-of-the-mill spoilt middle child, I never imagined I'd be where I am today. As a result of achieving affluence and emotional stability, I live a relatively privileged life now as opposed to my childhood, when all my traumas and struggles collectively pandered to the idea that substance abuse was the only escape from reality.

Today, I live a life filled with abundant blessings. I have a stable, functioning home and work life. Apart from that, I am someone who is highly concerned about the well-being of others and want to make a difference in their lives, probably because I can relate. I have a master's degree in Addiction Counseling, a master's in social work, and I am currently working on my Doctoral in Psychology. I'm a licensed Independent Chemical Dependency Counselor. I also own and successfully operate a treatment center for adult males who suffer from mental health and substance abuse. By shedding light on all of what I've achieved, I am by no means trying to toot my own horn, but rather giving you a glimpse into my life, to show you that anything is possible if you just believe in yourself. Everything is subject to change; with that in mind, never let failure stop you from hoping for a better tomorrow.

My life today is beyond amazing. I feel whole and complete as a person, but it wasn't always like this. I've seen my fair share of troubles. While growing up, my life was a complete disaster. My future seemed bleak. I remember getting into drunken brawls. I was often seen scuffling with other kids my age. From being homeless to experiencing domestic violence, I've experienced it all while I was only a kid. Naturally, I developed a rebellious persona. I got caught nicking on several occasions. I spent time in a juvenile center; I started drinking to the point of blacking out; I was pregnant at the age of 16. While most girls my age were getting through school, picking out college options, I was bringing a baby into this world. But looking back at my life today, I think my biggest struggle was my drug addiction.

You may be wondering how I managed to turn my life around. It takes a tremendous amount of grit, courage, and perseverance. I suppose deep down, I always knew things needed to be changed. I needed to believe in myself and in the fact that anything is possible, and that's exactly what I did. For the longest time, I thought my childhood was what bound me to drugs. The contrast between the smiles and happiness and the stone-cold stillness within me was jarring. I suppose the best way I could describe my life is that it often straddled the line between trust and recklessness. Before I go into further detail regarding how I went from serving time in prison to being engulfed in a series of emotional and physical trauma that started to shape my life, let me take you back right to the very beginning.

I was born to Layfield Sr. and Gladys Sampson on the 18th of September, 1972. We were four siblings, I being the only girl. I was the second oldest child. My elder brother Layfield Jr. was, for the most part, raised by my grandmother. I had another brother; his name is Rayfield. Rayfield was only a year younger than me. I was protective of my younger brother and would stand up for him when he couldn't stand up for himself, partially because I was an angry kid but mostly because I loved him, and perhaps a part of me felt responsible when it came to him since he was younger than me. It was when I turned nine years old that my parents gave birth to another baby boy—they named him Myrick. Our family was complete, but we had a dysfunctional household environment. It wasn't exactly the most peaceful home to grow up in. However, I can say this with full confidence that the love was there—we were just not very expressive.

I clearly remember doing household chores at an early age. I had learned how to wash the dishes, and I would help clean the house as often as I could. My mother needed the extra help since my father was a busy man. He was a trucker hauling logs. My father was a hardworking man. His main goal was to provide for the family so that we didn’t even have to struggle, and he was doing a pretty good job. My mother, on the other hand, was a stay-at-home mom. She had her hands full with three kids, looking after the house, cooking, and cleaning. My grandmother had Junior since he was a baby. I saw him often, but he didn't have to see a lot of the things the rest of us saw. I always envied him because I should have been with my grandmother too. They had an understanding, and it worked well for them.

I went to Frankford elementary school. It was a decent school, providing us with a sustainable environment. The teachers paid close attention to all students. Students were encouraged to take part in activities they would thrive in. I started out strong. I was good at school, never had trouble with my studies. The teachers never complained, and I had a good relationship with my classmates. I would get along with other students.

Things started going downhill when I reached fourth grade. All of a sudden, I was falling back. I was struggling to keep up with the work. This was the point in my life where trying to focus and getting through classes had become an arduous journey I had to go through every day until it became burdensome not just on me but also on my teachers. They started noticing how I was falling behind. Eventually, the school had to contact my mother. It wasn't exactly my proudest moment, but then again, there was nothing I could do about it. I had no idea why I was struggling.

Looking back now, the only thing that comes to mind is the dysfunctional home life. The emotional neglect that I went through was taking a toll on me and causing me to act out. My mother was an alcoholic, and my father was a workaholic. "My father did not drink", but he allowed a lot of things to happen in our household. I always felt like why did he allow her to treat me so badly. I guess I'll never know that question. I had developed this idea in my mind that this was a healthy way of life. I, too, experimented with alcohol at a very young age. I might not be able to pinpoint exactly what it was that was affecting my studies at that age, maybe it was a series of events piling up, but I failed fourth grade. I felt completely out of place. I suppose you could say that was the point from where my life went spiraling down. I had to repeat fourth grade again. It felt odd and affected my self-esteem seeing my classmates move onto the fifth while I had to stay back. I felt completely out of place. Fortunately, I managed to pass fourth grade the following year, and that too with flying colours. I moved onto fifth grade and did well. Probably because I was in Special-Ed, which made it significantly easy for me to focus on everything that was going on around me. Till fifth grade, I had my life and my emotions under control. It was when I moved to the sixth grade that my life began to change. I hope no one faces the struggles and challenges I have had to face.

Chapter 2

Colonial Estates

At ten, my family and I moved to 'Trailer Park Colonial Estates' that had a peaceful environment. The area was well kept, and most people living there were courteous and friendly. From what we heard, this place was free from any kind of violence, but the best part was that there were plenty of stores and supermarkets close by. Our every need was catered to easily because everything we needed was in proximity to the trailer park. There were a lot of kids my age who lived there, which made the location ideal for a 10-year-old.

As far as I know, we had a good life. We were living in a peaceful environment; my dad was doing well, providing for us. We never had too many expectations and were more than satisfied with what we had. It's one of those qualities that has served me well, being present to the moment. Although I am not proud to say this, my mother was the dope dealer of the neighborhood, which meant that she was never short on cash. She had everything she wanted, which included a nice burgundy Camaro. She was a functional alcoholic, which means she had a drinking problem;

there were days when she was binge drinking, but she was still seemingly to the world outside, functioning well. It looked like life was going on as it should be, but on the inside, something was definitely not right for her to be drinking as much as she did. I knew she had a drinking problem when I noticed she had a hard time relaxing and having fun without alcohol on board; she had lost the ability to enjoy the little things in life without the use of a substance. She just had a hard time stopping whenever she would start, often crossing the limits and boundaries she had set for herself. I often noticed she would wake up in a dazed state when she would blackout the night before and would be on edge after waking up because a lot of times, she didn't remember what she had said or done while drinking. Apart from that, she had everything in control.

My parents were socialites; they were a friendly duo; the neighbors were fond of them, and they had company on most weekends. They loved having friends over. I remember them having small gatherings at home playing card games with their friends. I could hear people talking loudly and laughing. It seemed like they were having a great time. My parents knew how to entertain their guests. I noticed the adults had an amazing time while drunk. Children mirror their parents or adults that they look up to, so naturally, I developed this idea that alcohol had something to do with them having a great time, and it was an essential part of having fun that led me to try out beer myself. It tasted awful, but my mind told me that it is what makes them happy, so I learned how to drink beer. My parents obviously were unaware of the fact that I was experimenting with alcohol. They never found out, and I was extremely cautious. I made sure I never got caught.

I remember this one particular night; my mother was in the house. She was fast asleep. It was a beautiful night. My mother had my grandmother's car. I don't know what I was thinking. The daredevil in me decided I was old enough to drive, so I looked at my younger brothers and told both of them we were going on a drive. I remember driving around the trailer park—what a rush. As far as I knew, I had total control. I was doing pretty well; I drove up to the main road and then to the other end of the trailer park. I don't know about my younger brothers, but I was having a lot of fun. I felt like an adult; I felt a sense of freedom; it was reckless, but I didn't care; I was absolutely sure that no one would find out until I lost all control and smashed into a tree. Luckily, no one got hurt. When I realized what had happened, my heart started pounding.

To make matters worse, a close friend of the family had heard the loud noise and came out to see what caused it. I knew for a fact I was in a lot of trouble now. I was terrified; I don't think I have been more scared than I was at that moment. If I'm not mistaken, my mother was immediately informed because the next thing I remember is that she came all the way to where we were, where we had crashed the car. We knew we were in trouble, but before I could read her expression, my mind told me to run, and that's exactly what I did. I couldn't face the consequences of what I had done, endangering my life. What scared me the most was the punishment I knew I would probably receive. I wasn't ready to face the butt whipping that I was going to get; the thought of it made me shudder, fear enveloped me, and so I did what any ten-year-old would do, I hid under my bed.

For hours, my parents kept looking for me. I thought I was safe under my bed until my brother Ray came into the room, bent down, and peaked under the bed; he yelled for my mom, saying, "mom, here she is." My heart started racing; I thought he was going to yank me out of there. I was trying to fend off tears and put on a brave face until my father walked in, lifted the bed up, and in a heavy assertive tone of voice, he said, "Get your ass up." That's one of those traumatizing days that has been embedded in my memory forever. I will never forget that day because I got whipping three times that day, first by my mother and father and then my grandmother. I know they meant well, and they were only trying to teach me a lesson for being reckless, but it was too much for me to handle. It emotionally scarred me. I was grounded, which meant I couldn't go outside for anything. I used to sit by the window looking outside, wishing for this punishment to be over.

My mom taught me many things; one of those things was washing my own clothes; I not only washed my own clothes, but I also had to wash my blankets and hang them outside on the clothesline. Washing blankets is not an easy task for a kid my age, but I had to do it because I peed on the bed. The reason I peed on my bed was because of stress. I understand that now, it had a lot to do with my lifestyle. There were unresolved issues in my mind that I didn't know how to deal with, and I didn't exactly have a mentor to help me understand what I was going through. Inner child wounds were being formed, and they just kept getting worse from there. I can proudly say that I have healed most of those inner child wounds over time, but some of them still haunt me to this day.

Things took a turn for the worse when I was 11 years old. Whenever I was around the trailer park, I just felt free. It was my happy place. I remember when I was young, things were good, to the world outside and my family, I was a cheerful kid. As I mentioned before, I was doing well in school. I wasn't exactly a delinquent; sure, I made mistakes like driving my grandmother's car and drinking alcohol but overall, I was a good kid, someone who was always trying to be the best version of herself, trying to be good at everything, trying to get good grades, although my home life was far from perfect, it was something I could cope with.

I lived a childhood of survival after one particular incident. I went to meet a friend of the family in the trailer park when I was sexually molested by him. I vividly remember when it happened. Like I said, I was only 11; he was much older than me, and it breaks my heart to say this, but I liked the attention he was giving me. I was unaware of the fact that what he was doing was wrong. By the time I realized what had happened was wrong, I was a changed person. I spent most of my time thinking if something like that could happen again, if I'm going to be pounced on, how do I stop it. It's not something you forget.

Over time, I just shut down. I wasn't my person anymore. I had developed fears that were rational and blanked through any traumatizing experience so that I could just carry on with my life as best as I could, but things didn't always go as planned as time went by, I started bottling up my emotions and eventually became extremely rebellious toward anyone who had an input in my life. I started acting out; I started getting into trouble at home more and more without caring about the consequences. I even started sneaking out of the house in the middle of the night, which I admit was dangerous, but it was the rebel in me that made me want to do everything that my parents would not approve of. Apart from that, I was often seen scuffling with other kids, challenging them to get into fistfights with the kids in the trailer park. I couldn't seem to get along with anyone, and I am pretty sure my parents and teachers were noticing this change. I wish someone had sat me down and asked me if something was bothering me, or at least given me the reassurance that I was loved and cared for; support, any kind of support, can do wonders for a kid who is struggling to find themselves. Unfortunately, I didn't have anyone to who I could talk, which led to me turning into a complete delinquent. I was out of control, and I knew it. Another terrible habit I developed, or like I used to say, a skill that I developed, was stealing from stores without getting caught. I didn't need to steal, and honestly, I don't know why I acted out like this. Perhaps I was punishing myself for something I had no control over. Or maybe I just needed to be seen. Maybe it was a call for help. It's a classic move by young children when they feel ignored or are abused. They resort to acting out.

I suppose one of the most valuable skills I developed as a child was learning how to make money. To some extent, it taught me how to be responsible. I started making money by doing some simple gardening work. All I really had to do was cut grass and rake leaves. It wasn't tiresome. In fact, it was quite simple, considering I was used to household chores. Raking leaves and cutting grass was a piece of cake and the money I earned was not too bad. It was more than enough for someone my age. I specifically remember this one older lady I worked for; I took care of her yard. She had a warm, gentle aura and was like a granny to all the kids. I enjoyed working for her; she was a wonderful lady.

She had two granddaughters who would visit her on holidays and on special occasions. I became close with her granddaughters. We became good friends, and I enjoyed their company more than anyone else's. I remember I used to keep asking their grandmother if the girls would be back soon. I was always waiting for them to visit their grandmother. They lived in Baltimore, Maryland; these girls are part of all the positive aspects of my childhood. I adored and loved them like they were my own sisters. I don't need to mention names; they know who they are. I just hope they know how influential their role was in my life, and I couldn't be more grateful for having such caring and loving friends like these two.

Chapter 3

Foster Care

By the age of 12, I started indulging in excessively prevalent unethical habits. My behavior could be deemed as reprehensible. I was attending Selbyville middle school at the time. I clearly remember the environment at school; it was pretty decent. It was around that time when I picked up a terrible habit; smoking. A good friend of mine would smoke cigarettes with me. I was a delinquent, and there was no question about it. I would do things that would infuriate my mother. She had had enough of me and called child services, and the state worker came and removed me from my home. When asked why she wanted me to be placed in foster care, her reply was disheartening. She said she feared physically hurting me. I saw her expression when I was being taken away; she had a poker face. She simply couldn't put up with my behavior, so I was immediately placed in foster care.

Before being placed in foster care, I remember this one time I was hanging out at the trailer park, and it was a pleasant day. The sun was shining brightly in the sky, there were several kids my age or younger playing outside, and a warm breeze whipped the area clean. I was sitting there, listlessly observing people passing me by when my eyes fell upon my brother. There was this other kid who was giving my brother a hard time. I felt this sudden surge of innate responsibility that comes from being an older sister. I walked up to him and asked him to leave my brother alone. I asked nicely, but he completely disregarded my request and was being smart about it. So naturally, I used the only arsenal at my disposal; my fist. I busted him in the head with a bicycle crank. I had no remorse; in my mind, I did the right thing. I stood up for my brother when he couldn't take care of himself.

I was the kind of girl who was constantly getting into arguments and fistfights with the other kids in the neighborhood. I had developed an astute, mean personality. I was someone who could be provoked easily; most kids steered clear of me. Those who supported me did so out of fear because I was the kind of girl who wouldn't take shit from anyone. There was so much rage building up inside of me.

I now understand why I was such an angry kid. Anger made me act out often, and yes, a lot of times, anger, much like fire, can be good, but it can be highly destructive the longer we hold onto it. Anger makes us react quickly and irrationally so that we can protect ourselves from potential danger. It's an automatic response when we feel threatened, more like a coping mechanism. When faced with the challenges I had to face, anger wasn't something I could control. I was always ready to fight. It's how I figured I'd survive. My brain would make impulsive decisions in a matter of seconds. A lot of times, the threats weren't even real or so minor that they could have easily been handled through an act of arbitration. But being calm seemed like an impossible task at the time. I needed to take the frustration out. I needed someone to give me a reason to let the anger out. I might have even reframed a story just to get into a fight. I can't be absolutely certain about that, but it is a possibility I wouldn't want to rule out because, like I said, anger makes us impulsive, and I was impulsive.

It wasn't long before I was placed in foster care. I was placed with a doting lady named Gerry; she adored me. She had an exceptionally pleasing personality. I was happy and felt content. Gerry raised me as her own. She already had two children of her own. They were both much older than me. While I was under Gerry's care, it was almost as if internal peace had been restored. Gerry went out of her way to make sure I was provided with a comfortable environment. She was extremely nice to me, and that is something I will never forget.

While I was under Gerry's care, I also had a foster sister. Her name was Toni. Toni and I were like two peas in a pod. We had a lot in common and subsequently enjoyed each other's company. Toni and I developed a deep bond. We hung out together all the time and even went to the same school. I was attending Woodbridge middle school in Bridgeville, Delaware, at the time. For those of you who aren't from the United States, Bridgeville is a relatively small town situated in Delaware. The town is known for its history, and you may even see travelers come by for specific events or holidays; it's quite a relaxing area. It is also a bit remote but not secluded. It's quite close to some large cities like Dover and Salisbury. The town, despite its size and population, was known for many things. My favorite thing about the town was the beautiful tree-lined streets that stretched on for miles, the malls, and the downtown alley.

Even though I loved being in Gerry's company, there were days I missed my home and family. I'd sit at night trying to fend off tears. I tried to appear composed. I didn't want anyone to think of me as weak. The anger inside me came from feeling abandoned, not fear or weakness. I suppose I just needed to be heard. Some of my friends weren't exactly a good influence. I don't blame them, though. They probably had troubles at home just like I did.

From time to time, I was able to go home and spend time with my family, but then after meeting them, I had to head back to my foster home. It was quite a hassle moving back and forth. I just wanted one place I could call home. The visits continued. I would meet my family and then head back to my foster home until, one day, things got out of control, and I got into a fight at school. It wasn't pleasant and resulted in immediate suspension. My worker came and, after assessing the situation, removed me from the home I was in. She left me in a state of confusion when I asked where we were going. She told me that I was going back home. That wasn't the case, though. I did not go home. Instead, she took me to my grandmother from my father's side. I was ecstatic, considering this was a woman who showered me with love; a warm feeling would envelop me whenever I was in her presence. I thought I had forgotten how to smile, but she reminded me what happiness was, and I found myself smiling and laughing again. The wrinkles on her face revealed her true nature, a gentle, loving soul. The best part about living with my grandmother was the homemade ice cream she would make for me. My grandmother was more like a mother to me. She did the little things that you would expect from a parent. I will always love her for taking me in and looking out for me. She shed light on several important things young girls should know about. She took care of me, spoilt me, loved me, and taught me what I needed to do when I hit puberty. It was my grandmother who showed me everything I needed to take better care of myself.

I should mention she wasn't living alone. My aunt and cousin lived with her. My cousin was much older than I was. I was fond of him; he was a joy to be around. It was funny how he was not allowed to drive the car or go anywhere unless he took me along, and I suppose that's how he and I bonded. He treated me like his own little sister. We used to hang out quite a lot. It would be me, him, and his girlfriend. He didn't mind me tagging along, and they never made me feel like a third wheel. In fact, he made sure I was having a good time.

As much as I enjoyed living with my grandmother, my aunt, and my favorite cousin, it did not last long. My mother was against the idea of me living with them. I'm not exactly sure why she didn't want me living with my grandmother. After all, she was the one who had sent me away in the first place. Nevertheless, she had me removed from my grandma's house.

I was thirteen years old when this happened. I moved back home, and that's when my personality took a turn for the worse. I became more defiant, and things at home were turbulent. I was wayward, and there was no stopping me. I started stealing items from local stores for no reason until I finally got caught stealing out of a teacher's purse in school. That's when serious action had to be taken. That's when I appeared in court for the first time. I felt my world crumbling down, but I knew I had to face the consequences of what I had done.

The punishment wasn't all that harsh, but for a 13-year-old, it was hard to handle. I was put on probation. I was sent to Seaford house group home. I absolutely dreaded being there. The air felt so heavy indoors. I did not want to be there at all. Being at the Seaford house group home is a memory embedded in my mind so deeply because of the emotional turmoil that came along with it. All I did was cry until one day I got this bright idea to run away. I thought it was a smart move, and so I teamed up with two of my friends, and we decided to go to their father's house and steal his truck along with some money so we could drive to Florida.

It really did seem like a brilliant plan until we were caught in a high-speed chase. So much for Florida. We ended up in Stevenson juvenile detention center. That was the worst time of my life. I never thought I'd end up in juvie. I was there for almost a month and then appeared in court, where I was sentenced to six months in Ferris school for boys and girls.

Once I completed my six-month term, I was sent to Texas to live with my grandfather and his wife. That's when alcohol became a problem. That's when I became addicted. I had easy access to alcohol, and I started drinking heavily. At the time, I was going to the army base (Fort Hood, Texas) with two friends who were like sisters to me. My grandfather was not fond of them. He had an aversion toward certain types of people. My friends were Vietnamese. My grandfather was in the Vietnam war. I guess seeing their faces brought about flashbacks. His attitude toward them was beyond my understanding, but it didn't matter, and I didn't care. He never passed a racist comment, and he never said anything that would hurt them. He was a good man, and I loved him.

During my time in Texas, my drinking habit got out of control. I was blacking out, completely hammered on most days. I drank so heavily that they had to put me on a plane and send me back to Delaware. I was completely wasted on the flight, coming in and out of consciousness.

Before I knew it, I was at the Philadelphia Airport, standing there waiting for the bus to get me home. The very next day, I was back in foster care. My mother had given up all hope. She did not want to be bothered with me anymore, and my dad did not stop her. Perhaps he, too, felt the same. He allowed all of this to happen. I should have expected it this time, but this is the kind of thing you never get used to. I went to a foster family in Houston, Delaware, just outside of Milford, Delaware. I was 15 years old at the time, and I was there with them till I turned 16 years old. A whole year had passed by. I guess I didn't notice how quickly the time had gone by simply because these people, my foster family, were incredibly nice to me. They treated me like I was their own kid. They did not differentiate; they loved me and took care of me. I was lucky because I have heard stories of how teenagers my age end up with families who mistreat them. Mine, however, was quite the opposite. They frequently brought cigarettes for me because I was in the habit of smoking. My foster mother taught me how to crochet. I made a blanket, which I gave to my mother.

When I reached 9th grade, I went to school at Milford High school and, surprisingly, got good grades. Something had changed; maybe it was the comfortable environment or the fact that my every need was being catered to. I was doing good in school. I even learned life skills like how to give her insulin. My foster mom was the perfect person to be a parent. I loved her so much.

My family permitted me to date this one boy from school. I lived about a mile from him, and he was slightly older than me, seventeen to be precise. He was extremely good-looking, and I was happy with him. I remember this one night I went over to his place, and we ended up having sex. It was probably then that I conceived, and I didn't even know it. I didn't think I would end up getting pregnant. I wouldn't have found out if it wasn't for my pesky brother. I was finally going back home with my parents. I made it home safely; I still had no idea I was carrying his child. It happened all of a sudden when I was casually lying on the floor watching TV. My brother was pestering me, asking me why I was sleeping so much. I snapped at him, saying, “Boy, leave me alone!” He didn't stop.

He went up to my mother, and then I heard him say, "Look at her stomach. She looks pregnant." Fear took over. I was terrified because I did not want to be kicked out of the house again.

My mother carefully observed and immediately said, "We will see the doctor tomorrow."

Long story short, I was three months pregnant. She insisted I have an abortion. I took a strong stance and said, "No." This baby would be the only person who was going to love me. The following week, I quit school and applied for a job.

Chapter 4

Potomac Job Corps

The next chapter of my life began with me at Potomac job corps in Washington DC in the year 1988; I had conceived—16 and pregnant—and around this time, I wanted to complete something to get my life back on track. The realization that I was homeless while pregnant at 16 years old when word gets around someone was bound to blow it out of the water, so I had to do something right for once. So I signed up to do business clerical; I would complete my GED and trade at the end of the day. I got familiar with the place in no time and started working on my GED and trade simultaneously.

While at the job corps, I met several people in my age bracket, and a favorable aspect of being pregnant was that many people found themselves being gravitated toward me. I met these two girls, and we became quite close; they always had my back and constantly looked out for me. Being the delinquent that I was, I couldn't help but sneak out of the campus. The three of us snuck out on several occasions to go downtown DC to see what it was like; we traversed through the busy streets. We would drink and have fun; we would do things that were amusing; we just wanted to be happy. I, for one, wanted to forget all my troubles and enjoy myself whenever we'd sneak out. Yes, I was pregnant and indulging in alcoholic beverages, primarily because, at that age, we were not quite aware of the effects it could have on the baby. I was ignorant in that regard; perhaps I would have taken certain precautions had I been aware of the consequences of drinking during pregnancy. There was no one around me who could have guided me on the dos and don'ts, so I just did what any teen would do, live my life, explore new things and do the things we were forbidden to do. Our curious nature gets the best of us. From what I remember, I was having a lot of fun.

Through it all, I managed to complete the trade-in four months but was still working on my GED; I was too hungover to make it to class every day. My head would be pounding, and all I wanted to do was sleep it off.

As time went by, my baby was growing, and things were becoming all too real for me. By the time I was eight months pregnant, I had to meet my counselor to figure out what I had needed to do and which path I'd be better suited for. Her guidance at this point was potent because I had to go home.

They could not keep a baby and me on grounds; it was too much of a liability. In the back of my mind, I knew I had to leave at some point; I didn't expect it to be so soon. Everything was starting to make me come to a realization that I was already a mother. You can't even begin to imagine how challenging and emotional my situation was at the time. I wanted the best for my baby. I just wished and hoped someone had guided me to a proper pregnancy resource center, where I could have received the help that I needed through this time. I wanted to be around people who would be caring and non-judgmental; I wanted someone to assist me without feeling sympathy or judging me for being in the position I was in. I also needed advice for the baby, what needs to be done. The right steps that I should be taking during the nine months and the steps I would need to take after the delivery, but it's unfortunate I didn't have anyone around me I could confide in when it came to the anger I had in me, the frustration, maybe even the loneliness perhaps I hadn't noticed it myself, I was too busy having the time of my life getting hammered with my two friends.

I sometimes wonder, had my brother not ratted me out, if he wasn't such a narc at that age, would I have the courage to go up to my parents and tell them myself that I was pregnant? I wonder if their reaction would have been the same as it was, utter shock, anger, and disappointment, I know my parents were not my enemies; they were not against me. It's just the circumstances didn't serve me well, and I can't blame anyone for that. As a parent now, I know how you want what's best for your child. You want them to do well in school; you want them to adopt good habits. I will encourage young teens to open up to their parents. If something in your life is off-balance, let them know about it before it consumes your entire personality. The pregnancy was tough, but I knew in my heart that my precious baby would love me beyond measure. The changes I needed to make in my life were for the sake of my baby; I wanted my child to have the kind of life I was deprived of, sadly. At the time, I had little to no control over my life, and most decisions were out of my hands. If you are wondering why it's because I was underage.

The day had finally arrived when my mom was called; a lady spoke to her informing her that they could no longer keep me due to the fact that I was carrying a baby. It was one of the saddest days of my life; I was completely devastated. My mother firmly told this lady that they needed to find another place for me to go; her exact words were, "She can't come here with no baby." The lady was in a tough position. She explained the situation, which only aggravated my mother to the extent that she hung up the phone on her.

I can't even begin to explain how I felt. I was trying my best to fend off tears. I did not want to cry in front of anyone; I wanted people to see me as a tough girl. Soon the day arrived when I had to leave Job Corps head home. I was provided with some money so that I could get home easily; they also gave me a bus ticket. I finally made it home safely.

Chapter 5

The Baby Girl

The ride to my parents' house was utterly dreadful. During the whole journey, I was just contemplating their reaction to the fact that I would be living with them, not only me but also my baby. They hadn't been exactly supportive of her and viewed her as a burden. All my dreams shattered of doing something right for once in life and standing on my own two feet. I was back to square one and worse off in some ways. I had a baby to support, and my delivery was in a few months. I couldn't even begin to imagine how expensive it would be. The delivery was just the tip of the iceberg. Providing sustenance, care, food, and education were only the main things. I did not know how I would manage all this under the disappointing eyes of my parents. My head began to throb, and I couldn't see any light at the end of the tunnel. I rested my head on the bus seat, closing my eyes, relishing the short-lived peace that I would be getting perhaps in a long while. I was prepared for the worst.

My bus stopped at the bus stop, and I looked around foolishly, thinking that my parents might have come to pick me up. I smiled to myself. How naïve I was! They didn't want me, and they made no secret about it. I needed to stop my wishful thinking. I stumbled from the bus stop carefully, holding the little belongings that I had, and looked around. Just as expected, no familiar face was in sight. At that moment, my heart broke a little. I understood that this was hard for my parents, too. It was a shock for them, but I needed them. Couldn't they put their arrogance aside and be there for me? I guess not, and I smiled again sadly.

I waited for a cab at the bus stop and soon got one.

"Where to, miss?" He eyed me incredulously, and I didn't appreciate his looks. I quickly told him the address. I didn't have the energy to think about his inappropriate looks. I was used to them by now; I heard the whispers as I passed by. I was a stereotype. They probably assumed all kinds of horrible things for me. It used to bother me at first, but now I didn't care. I was too tired to care, and I couldn't blame the onlookers either. I wasn't an exactly ideal sixteen-year-old, and people just needed to gossip.

The cab ride was uneventful and littered with my thoughts. I was feeling anxious as the distance got less and less. I didn't know how I was going to face them. I did not have the energy for drama, let alone fight with them. Or even worse, look at their disappointed faces.

The cab came to a halt, and I looked outside. The house

loomed over my head, and I sighed deeply. The trailer park was spread out, and all the memories went through over my head. I did not want to be here again, somewhere where I was never wanted, even when I was a kid. How will they accept me now, when I was more of a burden than ever I was before? I resented my mum more than my dad; he allowed her to exploit me in any that she wanted, and he just stood there silently. As I walked toward the trailer, I pledged that I would be the best mother this baby could ever get. This brought happy tears to my eyes and gave me strength.

I knocked and was given a hostile welcome. They didn't seem pleased to see me. Not that I expected them to, but I would have liked that. I went over to my old room and laid my things on the bed. Already I was feeling suffocated. This could not go on for long. I was lost and didn't know what to do. I thought that my mother would, in turn, allow me to come home, seeing that it was her first grandchild, but that was not the case. I felt very lonely during this process.

The next day I went hunting for places where I could stay and possibly a job, but no luck. I didn't want to find a new place to stay, but the atmosphere back home was not ideal. It was a spontaneous decision but one that needed to be made. Fortunately, a friend of mine was kind enough to let me stay over during a portion of the day. I was grateful to get away from the glare of my mum and my dad's indifference. It was like a breath of fresh air, and I relished every second of it. I was always sad when I had to go back to my parents'.

During these times, I had also met a man who was two times my age. In the beginning, I thought it was cute. I really liked him because he showed me attention; I thought that he really cared, but the truth is I never really knew who he was. His name was James, aka Junior. He was tall, with brown eyes and a brown skin tone. He also had a beautiful smile. I liked the idea of hanging out with him. He would take care of me, shower me with compliments even in my disgruntled pregnant state! I was over the moon and couldn't be happier. Soon I ended up moving to his place around the corner. It was so much better than my parents', and I didn't feel suffocated either. My pregnancy was also getting closer throughout this period, and I made regular visits to the doctor. When I went to the doctor, I had no one to go with me. I went alone to all of the appointments since I had made it back home to Delaware.

I was particularly concerned if my baby girl was in the ideal position to come out to the world, but unfortunately, she was as stubborn as her mother. My delivery date was May 15th, 1989, but there was a delay because my baby had decided that she did not want to come into the world on time. I was scared at the thought that the baby was coming as I was a baby myself. I wondered how I was going to take care of this little person; I knew I was going to love her. I felt like I needed her to feel like someone would grow up and love me.

Just as well, the world was not exactly waiting to welcome her, but I was, and I was going to give her all the love and care in the world. I went to the doctor again and got a date for a C-section. Having the thought of an operation was scary, especially with its stigma, but I was too naïve for my own good back then. It was the worst feeling in the world thinking about the operation, and it scared me to death, but it reaped huge benefits. From something scary, I got my beautiful daughter, and she was so incredibly pretty.

Even now, I don’t regret my choice. It should be the woman’s choice of how she wants her baby delivered, and also, I had no other choice than to get operated on. I got my hospital bag ready and got prepared for the operation. It felt so strange that I was going through this almost surreal phase in my life, and I had no family to support me. When did I grow up so much?

I was also fooling around with the older guy, who treated me like a princess, and on a whim, we decided to put his name on the birth certificate. Let's face it: I didn't even know who her dad was. But, at least this man treated her like his daughter and was ready to be her father even if she was not his blood. That thought comforted me immensely. He claimed her as his baby girl, and there was nothing I could do about it. My baby girl had a father who treated her well, and I could not ask for more. At the time, I was happy to have someone claim her because I could not think of who her biological father was at the time, and he showed care and love to this little girl. He told everyone that she was his baby, but we both knew the truth, he was not her father.

Chapter 6

Life of Drug Abuse

Life after a baby was different than I had perceived it to be; people were right in saying that a baby changes everything. I witnessed these changes myself. For the first seven months that my daughter was born, I was really happy. Life seemed perfect, and everything was easy breezy.

However, things soon started to change for the worse suddenly, after these blissful months. Junior's family used to visit every Friday after they got off work. They were making pretty good money, and they were chicken catchers. I had a strong gut feeling in my heart that they were mixed up in some shady business, specifically drugs. One by one, everyone would be clinging to pile up in the bathrooms. I watched from behind the shadows of doors and hallways, anxious to find out what was actually going on. I had this uneasy feeling in my heart, which made me desperate enough to find out the truth. And one day, I got my chance.

His cousin came in one day, looking for everyone. I informed her everyone had left, and she instantly went into the bathroom. I was quick on my feet and followed her, giving her a quizzical look.

"What are you doing?" I asked almost instantly. She denied everything and played innocent. I shoved her aside, knowing that something wasn't right. I had already seen her light up a pipe and smoke from it. As if the devil had possessed me, I snatched the pipe from it and took a whiff. I wanted to know what the hype was about. After that moment, my life changed forever.

Lighting that pipe was one of the single most regrettable decisions of my entire life. I later found out that I had taken my very first hit of crack cocaine. Boy, I was off and running after that; I was completely obsessed with the stuff. I just couldn't get enough and started to look for options where I could buy some besides Junior's family. Ultimately I had success when I found out a drug dealer right in my neighborhood. *What a blessing!* I had thought at the time. In actuality, it was anything but a blessing, I soon realized. I had become a complete strawberry, as I was ready to sell everything for drugs, ranging from shit to even my soul.

With time, my addiction became only worse. I had even stopped paying attention to my precious daughter - all I wanted to do was get high all the time. The drugs made me forget about the loneliness and pain I was feeling. The pain of my parents abandoning me, the responsibility of a small human being on my head, but most of all, I craved love. My daughter loved me, of course, but she was too small to understand the affliction I was going through. As far as I was concerned, they were my new friend.

I remember once I began craving the drug late at night. I thoroughly looked through my supplies, but I found none. I became so frenzied that I slept with Junior's cousin to possess the drugs from him. Unfortunately for me, Junior caught us in the act. He was furious, getting into a fight with his cousin. Then it was my turn. Next, he hit me into a surge of anger, and it hurt.

I went to my dad the next morning and told him everything. He didn't like the way Junior had behaved with me and threatened Junior. I still remember his exact words; they were something like this: "Put your hands on her again, and I would kill you." The very next day, Junior frantically began searching for another place to stay as he didn't want me near his cousin again. Also, he wanted to get me far away from the trailer park. He found temporary accommodation with another family member, and we went to stay there for a bit. I was completely new to the area and knew no one around me. One night, out of whim and in his drunkenness, he started to beat me. He beat me until I couldn't get up; I remember wishing that my dad was there right then. He would have taught him a lesson, but it was all wishful thinking. No one came to help me. His family turned their faces refusing to even recognize me. I guess empathy was not their style. However, I pledged to myself that this was the last time he was pounding me, and it did not happen again, at least not in Delaware.

About a month later, he came to me and talked about moving to North Carolina; he wanted the baby and me to move in with him as well. For some reason, I was excited about the thought of moving to a new place, and I readily agreed. It felt like a new start for me, where I could get away from all the drugs. Little did I know how naïve I was; Lord knows that nothing changed in North Carolina. Only the place was new; the circumstances weren't.

We stayed with his sister when we reached North Carolina. She had two kids of her own. Her son had a girlfriend living there and a baby who was about the same age as mine. That night we left the baby with his sister so we could go meet some more of his family members. However, just like always, things soon started going south within two weeks of us being in NC. He was arrested soon enough for something that he had done in the past. I was so frantic, and I don't even remember what it was that sent him to jail. I was all alone there when this happened; nevertheless, my baby was with his sister, who I knew would keep her safe and sound.

I got into my old habit again; I started to drown and held onto the drugs for dear life. It was worse this time, as I knew no one here, and even James was in jail, which meant that I had to find a new drug dealer completely on my own. This also meant that I was struggling for money for the drugs. Once I was caught stealing by the cops as I was trying to cash in a man’s check that I had stolen. I wouldn't have been caught if the lady who I had been getting high with hadn't told on me. She had witnessed everything, as it happened in front of her, and she was always given fifty dollars for being a witness to my crime. So I guess it was a win-win for her; she would probably use that money to buy more drugs. I, on the other hand, was scared and alone as I cursed her under my breath. Was there no empathy left in anyone these days? I guess everyone was just looking out for their own gain. I did not know what was going to happen to me. Luckily I called his sister to look after the baby until I got home. I was forever grateful to his sister while I was busy getting high and arrested; at least I had the comfort that my baby was alive and well.

I didn’t stay long in jail, probably a week or two max, after which I got out. I was lucky that the duration was not long. However, being imprisoned brought with it its own repercussions. My mind and body were completely dominated by the idea of getting high all the time in prison. However, I obviously did not have access to any. I found my solitude in drugs because the world and its people did not give me any. I just wanted to get high to take away any pain that I was feeling. I had a rough life after the first day of getting high. My life changed for the worse. I was running around like I didn't have a care in the world. My daughter was with James's sister and her kids, so I didn't have to worry about my baby because I knew she was being taken care of. That left room for me to do what I wanted to do, and I relished that thought.

Soon after, I was reunited with my baby. However, my drug addiction only increased. I still left my baby with his sister, even though technically I was the mother, and I should have taken care of her. However, I was too busy enjoying my life as a drug addict. The responsibility of a baby was too much for me, and my new obsession was prioritized first.

I met a lot of interesting people in my life, including a prostitute. She showed me the ropes of her work and, most importantly, the art of making money for myself, not for any pimps. Her name was Judy, and she was well known for her profession, in which she made a lot of money, and I desired to make money like her. She taught me the basics: set my price and not to lower it for any man. She advised me to stand firm, and if that price is not met, I should walk away; I should not let any man take advantage of me just because I was a woman. These tips were very helpful for the future. Even though I did not plan on becoming a prostitute, it comes with the territory of getting high on drugs. There's just this immense desire to get high that makes you do anything to survive.

On and off, I went to James's sister's house to check up on my daughter to make sure she was doing okay. One day I found out that she had moved out of the house and had taken my daughter with her; I was devastated. James came to see me; he had gotten out of jail by now. I asked for his help to get my daughter back. With his help, I was successful in getting her back, and all three of us started living together again in an old guy's apartment.

One night after I had gotten my daughter back, he came into the apartment drunk, yet again. He flipped out on me again, and thoughts came into my mind as I remembered the last time he did that. He beat me black and blue. Well, this time around, he beat me again, and moreover, he told me he was going to kill me. He went on further and said that I did not have my daddy to save me now, and he will make sure that I died that night. He was very drunk and reeked of alcohol. That night I felt truly terrified. I had made a lot of stupid decisions throughout my life, but this one had taken the lead. I was scared for my and my daughter's life. However, a glimmer of hope came into my eyes as I saw that he was getting tired and was getting ready to rest. I got up steadily and started a fire on the stove. I put up a pot on the stove and boiled a concoction of bleach, lye, and dish soap. While the mixture was boiling, I packed the few belongings that we had and called a cab. When the cab arrived, I took my baby and clothes to the cab and told the driver that I had forgotten something in the apartment and

I would be right back. I went back to the house and threw the boiling hot potion at him as I ran for dear life. I instructed the cab driver to take us to Greyhound, where we would board the bus back to Delaware.

We reached home safely; however, the very next day, a highway patrol came knocking at our doors. They were looking for me back in North Carolina for the man that I had scalded, and I was facing attempted murder charges. Sadly, I went back to NC and was sentenced to one year in Raleigh at the woman's prison. I was hopeless after I got arrested; life didn't seem to give me a break at all, and I just couldn't take it anymore. I was in tears when the judge sentenced me. However, a plus side of going to prison is that your sentence is reduced to half if you have served prison time before. This is something that I newly discovered, and I rushed back to the judge to talk to her. To my surprise, the judge completely dropped the charges, stating that they dropped down to an assault, and James had past records with the police against him from me. These were all the times I had called the police on him because of his habit of beating me.

Furthermore, the judge added that he was freeing me but only on one condition that I would leave the state of North Carolina and never come back. It was obvious that I didn't belong here, and I desperately wanted to go back home. Back in Delaware, my daughter was with my mother, who made sure she was taken care of while I sorted out my situation. I missed her so much. I hopped onto the bus and was back in Delaware in a jiffy. I collected my daughter from my mother, and both of us moved to Milton, Delaware. It was yet again a new start, and I was hopeful that this time it would be different. I felt like my life was in a rut, and I just couldn't get out of this toxic cycle. Truth be told, I wasn't actually trying to get out of the cycle either. I guess I was not over my addiction yet and didn't want to help myself. Deep down, I knew that this path would only lead to destruction, but I was too high to listen to that part of myself.

Chapter 7

Dirt Road

I had decided to move to Milton, but I required a lot of help; it was not easy to move from one city to another. Especially when you're broke with no financial support from anyone, even my parents didn't support the idea. My mother didn't like the idea of us moving away again; strangely, I thought she had gotten close to my baby girl. Even though I was pleasantly surprised, things had changed after her previous staunch belief of even acknowledging her. As much I liked the idea of my mother getting along with my daughter, I wasn't ready to let go of the drugs, which would be completely prohibited in my parent's house, and I honestly couldn't get enough of the drugs. I was completely addicted, and it was not as if I hadn't seen my fair share of troubles, which were brought on me several times by drugs used as well, but I guess I was too far gone at that point.

I managed to steer clear by a small margin every time I was saved by some small miracle which ordinarily would have knocked the socks off ordinary people, but no, not me; I lived as if I didn't have a care in the world. What I didn't realize was that I was jeopardizing my daughter's future for my drug escapades, but I was too naïve to realize it then.

I found a guy to help me move to Milton; Lord knows I couldn't do it alone. I moved there trying to woo him; he was good to me. And at that time, I needed someone to show me kindness. I wasn't aware of what I was looking for; I just wanted to get high and get past the pain and hurt that I had endured. I was a lonely being, praying to God to take my life away. I was aware that I had something to live for. However, things weren't going exactly as planned. My life was skyrocketing out of control, and I didn't know how to fix it. I felt like a twelve-year-old who got caught stealing, and no one offered support or care. No one ever taught me how to love myself, maybe because no one ever loved me. I was aware of my feelings toward my daughter. However, at the time, I was not a good fit for her, and she didn't give me a good enough reason to stop doing what I was doing.

I met him interestingly in Georgetown, and to my delight, he loved drugs too. We went together to buy drugs from a dealer and grew a friendship when smoking crack together. I didn't realize that there was a social life with the buying and selling of drugs, and soon another guy liked me. So much so that he became a frequent visitor. He was infamous around the area, and he used that to impress me. It was as if history was repeating itself, and when he invited me to live with him in his house, I readily agreed. My daughter was about three or four years old, and we needed a proper place to stay, which didn't qualify as a motel or abandoned house. I was happy with the prospect of living with someone who was also attracted to me; this made things easier at first, at least. My experience with James started the same way, but it turned into a mess in the end. I feared that prospect, but I was always desperate to find a new and clean place for myself and my daughter, and this seemed like the only available option looming over my head. Unfortunately, I wasn't financially capable of funding a house or even a room for my daughter and me. Moving to Milton now seemed like a bad idea, but I also had to get away from my mother. This was the only choice I was comfortable with, hoping that he would not turn out like James.

It was all good with this guy for a while until he started tripping. He became manic and dangerously possessive, and jealous. He thought some other guys were trying to get to me, which would make me move away from him.

Things were spinning out of control so fast that I barely had time to think over my decisions. I was going with the flow, living a carefree life, not caring about the repercussions of my decisions or how they affected the people around me. The only thing that I had time for was getting high; I began to neglect my daughter again, which attracted attention from other people who considered me unfit to raise a child. Two sisters, whom I met while living in Milton, became seriously concerned about my situation. A baby, drugs, and prostitution to get more drugs didn't add up. They considered me unsuitable for raising a child, and one of the sisters ended up taking away my daughter. However, they ended up becoming my friends, and I agreed to let my daughter live with them; I couldn’t have them around this insanity. And I knew in my heart that they would take better care of her than I ever could.

She had children of her own and thought it would be a good idea to be around other children. Immediately I agreed, as it gave me more freedom to run around and live life on my terms. I could do my thing without worrying about my daughter's welfare; I was sure she would be well taken care of while I embarked on my adventures.

One night when the guy came home, he seemed upset and started to accuse me of ridiculous things, which didn't make sense to me at all. He was acting utterly crazy; upon inquiring what was wrong with him, he said that he knew what I was doing. He implied that I had been using him. I fired back that we are not in a relationship, and it was simply a living arrangement that you graciously offered to us. Instead of talking rationally, he got angry and started hitting me without any warning. He had already been abusive both mentally and physically; this was one of the reasons why I sent my baby girl away.

However, I was not the same person who used to get beaten up by James all the time, and he used to get away with it. I was actively fighting him back as I was no one's punching bag, especially after being in an abusive relationship in the past. I was no longer going to stand for this. The final draw came when he hit me in the head with a jack, the one that is used to raise a car up when it needs fixing. I eventually left him after that and was glad to put all the drama behind me. I packed up the little things I had brought with me and ended up on the road, where the drugs and money were plentiful.

However, soon enough, I met another guy who had a twin brother. They were both so cute. However, I got cute to one guy, and we would perform sexual favors for each other while doing drugs and smoking crack. In the middle of this upheaval, I got pregnant again and was not even aware of it. However, when I did learn about the pregnancy, it only made me sad as I wouldn't say I liked the idea of being tied down again. I was already doing a terrible job at raising my daughter. Absolute strangers were raising her, and for most of the day, I didn't even know where she, I was too busy getting high at strange places, incapable of even taking care of myself. I was poorly capable of managing a second one;

somewhere in the back of my mind, I considered stopping selling my body for drugs as it was only making me pregnant, which I could not afford to at this stage.

I didn't know how long I was going to waste my life away on drugs. There was no set plan, but there were also no brakes stopping me until this pregnancy. So it was no surprise that I was overjoyed when the doctor informed me that the baby was stillborn. I went off and ran again as I had no one to answer to. Looking back, I feel like I had been obsessed by some drug lord; I couldn't get enough of the drugs. I was willing to do anything to get drugs in my system, even though they were not doing any favors for my health and wellbeing. To be honest, I didn't know how bad my health was, as I never had time for a doctor while I was living on those streets. All I knew was that I would get so high that I was ready to do anything to survive, especially during nighttime in the streets. The drugs were the solution to everything, and I considered that they would cure me of all my ailments. The only time I had gone to the hospital was to have a stillborn baby that I wasn't even aware of. Additionally, I had gone at the suggestion of a friend, who told me to get prenatal care or else the baby would die since I was jacking my system with drugs all the time. When I found out that the baby was dead, I took it as a sign from God signaling that I didn't need another baby. This was ideal for me because as soon as I left the hospital, I went back to the streets and the drugs. They still had to remove the baby from my body, and I felt the pain all over again. I was all alone and went through the process completely isolated. My parents had no idea that I was pregnant, as I didn't want them to think less of me than they already did.

One night I got into a car and smoked until I passed out. When I came to my senses, I didn't know how I got into the car and whose car it even was. It just satisfied my need for a place where I needed somewhere peaceful to do drugs, and I had found the perfect place. I wasn't alone in the car; I was surrounded by strangers, who I didn't know any better than exchanging a mere hello and the shared interest of drugs that united us.

While we were driving around, getting high, I noticed something in the woods. At first, I thought it was just my eyes playing a trick on me, as I was already high, but it happened again, and this time I was sure that there was something out there. I quickly informed the other people in the car that something was moving outside. However, they didn't take me seriously and thought that I was tripping. I shrugged it off and settled back in my seat, muttering "Whatever" under my breath. However, ten minutes later, my suspicions were visualized as nine millimeters were in front of us on our heads, commanding us to put our hands up and surrender immediately. It was the cops, and they were in the woods. I had been right all along, I thought smugly as I looked over at the other passengers in the car. I communicated with my face that they should have listened to me earlier, and I wasn't crazy, as they had assumed. I loudly proclaimed that next time you would all listen to me, and I was not crazy. It was a moment of proudness for me, but it was short-lived because we had all gotten caught, and the police were standing over our heads. The outcome was that we all ended up being in jail, which made sure that I was off the dirt road, at least for a while.

It was as if God had rescued me from myself. I wanted to be free from the lifestyle that I was living, as I had missed death quite a few times narrowly. I had begun to sell drugs for the Puerto Ricans who used to come down the dirt road; that was the main spot for all the drugs selling. I made some real connections with them, so much so that they began to trust me to bring them their money, and the best part was that I was getting high for free. I was okay with this arrangement until a buyer came through to buy some drugs and pulled off with dope. I nearly missed getting run over by his car. This incident left me shaken to my core because I could have gotten severely hurt. This was when I realized that a change needed to come; otherwise, I would die in the streets.

After I had gotten arrested by the cops, there were no drugs for me for a long while, and I wasn't happy about the idea of living day to day without drugs, even though prison ensured that I had a roof over my head and I wasn't living like a nomad, shifting from door to door. I ended the dirt road.

Meanwhile, word had spread back home that I had been arrested and that my daughter was not with me. My mother, who had already been upset with how I managed things, took advantage of the situation and immediately came to Milton to collect my daughter, where I had abandoned her with the two sisters. She severely disapproved of my choices, especially the way I was raising my daughter. However, to my surprise, she began to stay with her, took care of her, fed her, and put her in a school so that she could finally have a stable life which I was unable to provide for her my entire life. My mother was finally stepping up, and I had mixed feelings about this; I didn't know what to make of it.

My entire life, she had neglected me. Yes, I had my issues, and I was not perfect, but rather than with my issues, she abandoned me until I became wayward and figured things on my own. I was choosing to live my life whichever way I wanted. Most of the bad things that happened to me could have been avoided if I had just been offered support and compassion from my parents. I would have never had to move with James if they had just welcomed me home when I was pregnant with my baby girl. Come to think of it, it was most likely that I wouldn't have even gotten into my addiction to drugs if I had just a loving home to come to. And now, suddenly, she was ready to stand up for my daughter, magically appearing like a fairy godmother to rescue her.

As much as I appreciated her sentiments and the fact that she took care of her while I was locked away in prison, there was still a lot of resentment buried underneath, brewing and waiting to pour out. I had already decided that once I got out of prison, I would take my daughter back with me, but other thoughts were also haunting my mind. She was offering my daughter a better life, something which I can never offer to her, at least not in my current lifestyle. If I was going to take care of my daughter, I had to make some big changes in my lifestyle, which I was not ready to make. Frankly, after giving it a lot of thought, I realized I should let my ego and resentment slide and just let her take care of my daughter as long as she wanted, for both our sakes. My daughter would be better off with her, relative to how she had been living with me as I had abandoned her to strangers. Another plus point was that she would live with family, and I could visit her whenever I wanted, without the lingering worry of her well-being. Yes, it seemed like a smart decision to let her stay with my mother for the time being, at least until I got my life sorted.

Chapter 8

Wilmington Delaware

My life as a detainee was relatively uneventful until I transferred to the Baylor Women's Correctional Institution. I was sent there for stealing from the store to supply my habit. From a very early age, I had depended on myself to fulfill my needs. I was a go-getter, as my mother had always taught us to go after what we wanted, and that thought had stuck with me throughout my life. I had always been independent, which hasn't always been ideal for me, but it made sure that I knew how to survive.

I ended up in prison for stealing, and that's how I moved to Wilmington. I had no place to go and stayed from pillow to pillow, also known as couch surfing. Gradually I also went back to using drugs; there were no questions about it. I knew in my heart and soul that I wasn't ready to stop the drugs altogether, even though I had been taught enough lessons that highlighted the repercussions of using drugs. My stay at the prison turned out to be quite delightful, as I knew many people who were imprisoned from my time on the streets. This seemed like a mini-vacation compared to living on the dirt road; the only downside was that I wasn't allowed to use drugs. During my time on the dirt road, I stayed on the streets, moving from one abandoned house to another. All of these came with their own set of challenges that I had to navigate; coupled with acquiring drugs and finding food, I was living another level of crazy. However, the prison was so much calmer relative to what I was experiencing.

I resided in dorm five until I was transferred to dorm three. I started working with a recycling company during my stay; they required workers and nominated the ladies from the institution to function. There were many upsides to working at the company while in prison; number one was that it paid good money. For the first time in my life, I earned through honest work, not using any illegal methods to make my living. Additionally, I didn't have anyone back at home to send me money, and this was God's blessing. Otherwise, I would have had my hands tied during my stay at the prison. When I was outside, I was free. I knew how to make ends meet to survive, but this was different. There was no other way to earn until it was through the rules of the prison. However, this sudden improvement in my life was short-lived; as soon as I was out of prison, this source of financing ended. And I went back to my routine habit of using drugs and making money through that.

I went back. However, this time, I became pregnant with

my third child. However, it took a long time for me to register that I was pregnant. At the time, I was using my body for drugs, and it took me a while to realize that I had gotten pregnant due to a condom breaking. Also, he was a Mexican guy, and I knew nothing about him, including his name.

And to make matters worse, he was long gone before I could tell him I was pregnant with his child. I couldn't even remember properly until the baby was born, and I saw the baby's skin complexion, and it hit me. I had slept with the Mexican, as I had a gut feeling in my stomach that he was not entirely black, but I couldn't pinpoint my finger at his actual ethnicity. However, when I gave birth, it all became crystal clear suddenly. I had slept with the Mexican for money, and the consequence was right in front of me.

While I was in prison, I met this girl who treated me like a princess. I liked her; she was very sweet and loveable. She treated me with respect and care, something I had never been offered before, and wanted to build a life with me. At first, part of me didn't care about what people would say; nothing else mattered as long as I was happy. Suppose I was content with my life; who cares what other people thought? I had spent my entire life doing what I pleased and not listening to anyone else. When have I ever watched what other people had thought about me? To be honest, I didn't exactly fit the definition of a standard sixteen-year-old girl. My entire life, I ran amok making my own decisions without the guidance of anyone. My parents had shunned me from a young age, which was part of why I had turned out the way I did. I was like a wild creature running in the woods, doing my best to survive without a care in the world. Finally, I decided I would be happy for once in my life, and if my happiness was destined with her, then that's exactly what I was going to do.

During this process, I made a good friend who wanted to help me with my baby when he was born. My baby would be a boy; I had found that out recently when I visited the doctor. I was thrilled that I was going to have a boy since I already had a girl. However, I still had mixed feelings. I hadn't proven to be a good mother to my daughter, and who was to say that I wouldn't be applying the same behavior to my son. My new friends were beneficial to me during the total tenure of my pregnancy; she made sure that I ate, and she also got clothes for the baby. Months later, my delivery date arrived; however, I was still in prison. It was time to have my baby, and I was taken to Christiana Hospital, accompanied by one of the correctional officers. I had another C – section by God's mercy, which I don't know how I survived, and my son was finally born on July 3rd, 1995. He was such an adorable baby, literally the cutest baby I had seen in my entire life. And to think that I had just delivered him brought me immense joy. As the days progressed, he lived with my friend, as I still had to complete my sentence.

A few months later, I got out of prison and was dismayed to witness that someone had blindsided my friend. This was another person who I had loved and respected, who I had sent to court to take my son from my friend's mother–in–law. In hindsight, I thought she was trying to take custody of my son from me. However, the truth couldn't be far from this assumption. The lady had done a tremendous job in raising my son, and she had loved him like he was her very own. Anyway, when I went to court, the judge granted me custody of my son again, and I was finally free to take him back home with me. My excitement was at the highest level, and I had even found an apartment for us to live in.

However, shortly after getting out of prison, I was sent back to it for violating my prison. I had to send my son again to live in another one of my friend's places. However, she promised that she would bring him around often to see him and even spend time with him. Unfortunately, I got fooled once again, and she began treating my son like her property. She even stopped his visits and would not let me see him. To this day, I have feelings of resentment toward her, as she had tried to take advantage of my situation and take my most precious possession away from me. I found it harder to forgive and forget about the whole situation;

things were harder for me than others. So I stopped trying altogether; I went on with my life because I knew he was safe and well taken care of. I went back to my wild lifestyle.

One day, I was sleeping in one of the abandoned houses. My life was still very cut-throat, and I was doing anything I could to survive the belly of the beast. Suddenly I heard someone calling my name, and I began to peep through the windows as I was startled and scared at the same time. It turned out to be my older brother; I went out for a moment as I was glad to see him, but not how I was looking or feeling. He just came to check up on me, and for that, I would be forever grateful.

Over time, I met another guy, and we ended up becoming good friends. He found me attractive. Additionally, he also had a habit and was a little dope boy. We used to run the streets together, and I had also met his parents. Life was fun. This friendship eventually turned into a relationship, and we used to help each other out while in those streets. It was some twisted version of Bonny and Clyde. Some months later, I found out that I was pregnant again. However, I could not carry the baby as the news was broken to me through a miscarriage. The baby was five months old, and I could name him. It was heart-breaking to see one of my kids go away like this. Also, he was the birth child of a loving relationship, which made it so much more heart-wrenching.

They put him in a box and disposed of him. Suddenly, a thought hit me out of the blue that made me question my entire existence. I didn't know what I was doing with my life; I was just throwing it all away for a few minutes of pleasure. And it wasn't as if I hadn't suffered because of my lifestyle; believe me, I had. I had seen it all, all kinds of abuse, mental, physical, emotional. You name it, I have probably gone through it. And this should have been a wake-up call for any sane person, but I guess I wasn't the same one. I needed to take my life under my control, but I didn't have the guts to do anything about it. This incident hurt a lot, but it still wasn't enough to stop me from changing my lifestyle. We were still doing drugs, getting that money, smoking, and getting higher than the sky.

One day I was hanging out with one of my friends at her house while my boyfriend was at his parent's place. While hanging out in the backyard and the street, I stumbled upon an ounce or two of cocaine, and surprisingly, I knew who it belonged to. I called my friend, and both of us looked at each other fearfully. However, we took it and ran the neighborhood for the day. We made money out of it, even though it wasn't ours, to begin with. Little did we know we were brewing up a hurricane and not a gentle one at that. The guy to who the cocaine belonged found out what we had done and spread the word around. He paid people to beat my friend and me, and one particular day my friend got jumped. They knocked his tooth out and beat his ass all day behind me without my knowledge. Later that day, as things progressed, a guy attacked me as well and broke my jaw. I was so scared I didn't even tell people the truth; if anyone asked, I said I had damaged it during a car accident. I didn't want anyone to know the truth, as it would only make things more dangerous. These were some crazy things taking place, and for the first time, I was scared for my life. Breaking my jaw wasn't enough for him, and he had everyone around town beat me up as soon as they found me. I had to get away from that part of the town, or I would end up dead.

After my escape, my life began to spiral out of control, and I ended up at a hotel smoking with strangers. While smoking with these people, I learned about an organization that traveled all over the country selling books and magazines. This new prospect gave me hope, and I thought that finally, I would be able to get away from the drugs and my nomadic lifestyle. However, it turned out to be quite the opposite; my life pretty much remained the same. I was still doing all kinds of drugs and still living from door to door. I still didn't have a permanent address. So I took my dog and pony show on the road and ventured into my new life. I left with the only clothes that I was wearing on my back and headed off to New Jersey as I wanted to start making money right away. Surprisingly, I was good at selling books and magazines and made a number relative to the people who had been doing this gig for quite a long time. I was making my daily quote and getting paid nightly, ensuring that I never went to bed hungry and had a small budget for other things. However, as far as drugs were concerned, I was still steadily following the same route, in fact, now I had money to support my habit, and my daily frequency of drug usage increased. Eventually, the group ended up moving to Ohio from New Jersey, and I traveled with them.

My life was again moving very fast; I had little to no control of what I was doing. I just followed the current and ended wherever it threw me. I had escaped the town and left my boyfriend behind, but I was again to blame for that. If I hadn't been such a smart alec and hadn't sold the cocaine, which didn't belong to me, none of this would have happened. I had a pretty stable life with him and even some sort of parental love from my boyfriend. My situation had become so dire that I couldn't even afford to say goodbye to him. It saddened me, but there was nothing I could do; I couldn't risk my life. Otherwise, there would be nothing left to enjoy, especially the drugs. I don't know; I guess I was living my life in some sort of haze that stopped me from coming to my senses. What did I expect? That my life would be just going on this way forever, and it would be a bed of roses. I knew my life had been anything but that; if I had been living an everyday life up to the standards of everyone around me, maybe I would have suffered less. Maybe my parents would have accepted me, but then would

I have been happy? I wouldn't be doing any of the things that brought me joy. My parents' ideology of living one's life was opposite to mine, and I didn't expect them to understand my struggles. Maybe if they had just listened, I wouldn't have ended this way.

Chapter 9

Ohio

My journey to Ohio was relatively uneventful, and thank god for that. I think I have had enough adventure to last me a lifetime; little did I know that more escapades were waiting in store for me.

Once reaching Ohio, we instantly started working. We stayed there only for a few days before stopping at a place called Licking County. Yes, the name is funny, I laughed wholeheartedly when I heard it for the first time too, but it was nothing compared to how strange the place itself was. All of us started working immediately again after reaching there, and it was one of those particular days that I had a good turnout.

I was selling magazines at this lady's house when lady luck smiled at me, and she left the door open while leaving her purse behind. My eyes glittered at the prospect of money, and I swiftly stole her credit card and some cash she had. Then, after reddening my hands with the crime, I pranced toward the van as I couldn't afford to get caught. I had sworn to myself that I was never going to go back to prison, that life wasn't for me, even though it made me a better person in some regards. But the irony was that I was doing the exact things that would guarantee a place for me in a prison cell.

I stayed at cheap hotels during this time around, as I was tired of the dirt road life and craved a roof over my head. Deep down in my gut, I had a feeling that I would surely be going to jail after this, but I still took the risk. I paid for the room through her credit card, leaving a marked trail for the police to capture me. The police came in the morning to arrest me, banging on my door waking me up from my deep slumber. I did their work for them when I used the credit card, making it easier to track me. They arrested me for credit card theft and burglary, transporting me to Licking County jail. The only thing worse than being in Licking County was being in Licking County jail, and I hated and loathed every minute of it. The people I worked for were baffled that I had committed a crime; I was more saddened to hear that they were leaving the next day for another place. If only I had controlled myself and not committed the crime, I would have been able to escape this place. However, I was doing many stupid things, and I guess this one was right up my alley as well. It was nothing unexpected. I borrowed their phone to call my parents, so they would be informed of where I was and how I was doing. Meanwhile, I waited in jail, awaiting my sentence; I had to wait for a week before the court was ready to punish me. My punishment was a long one, one whole year in the Ohio reformatory for women.

I felt extremely broken after hearing my sentence. I was back where I had started; it felt like I was going around in circles. At this point, this is what my entire life summed up to, a hamster just running on the wheel, not knowing when to stop. I guess I was behaving like a hamster too, I had an active choice not to repeat my chances, but I guess I was forced by habit. It wasn't easy to break habits; even if I tried, I would repeatedly stumble upon the same path. As if my evil vices were calling out to me, making it harder for me to quit. I prepared myself mentally for what was to come, and even though I had been to prison before, it was nothing like what I was going to face now. I was kind of scared for my life and my fate. I didn't know what would become of me if I kept getting in trouble at this rate. My life was a complete mess and was becoming even messier day by day.

Within the next few days, I got accustomed to my new home for a year. This was the big league for me, and I didn't know what would happen from here on out. I just knew that I was in a miserable situation again, without any support, and would have to bear this all alone. I was glum primarily about not having access to drugs; my life was going well. I was getting high and selling magazines. I was living the glam life of a drug addict and enjoying every moment of it. If only I wouldn't have been naïve enough to steal her credit card and then actually use it. I wrinkled my forehead, thinking hard, and sighed deeply; nothing could be done now. I have been sentenced and will have to go through it now; regretting it now was no use.

My first day at the reformatory facility was horrifying, and I think I wouldn't forget that day till my last breath. We were admitted into a vast white room located in a huge building. Uniformed orderlies asked us to strip down from the uniforms we were wearing, that too, in front of everyone so they could check us thoroughly. I was stripping my clothes, but I felt I was being stripped of my dignity. I was so scared, I just kept to myself and told what I was supposed to do.

Moreover, we were instructed to put our hair down. If we were wearing braids, we were asked to open them up, and our nails were cut off. They made sure that we were not hiding anything that could potentially be used as a weapon. Next, we were ordered to shower with scalding hot water and sprayed down for bugs. It was the most harrowing experience that I had, and since I had been to prison before, I knew what I was talking about.

I was placed in a dorm with hundreds of other inmates, women of all kinds and who had committed all kinds of crimes as well. We had murderers, thieves, people who had committed arsenal, offenders for minute crimes such as shoplifters. All of them holed up together in one uncomfortable room. We were all assigned to numbers, and this is how the guards used to address us. I felt our identity was stripped, and we got accustomed to numbers rather than the guards calling out our names. Both the initial process and stay at the reformatory facility were soul-crushing. Once I completed half of my sentence, I was transferred to Franklin pre-release to complete the other half of my sentence. It was relatively good there than at the reformatory, and I was finally a little relaxed as I was heading to the end of my sentence. While I was in the pre-release, I found a pen pal who kept me company, and we became good friends. We used to write daily to each other, and it was wholesome to have finally found a friend. I was getting out before him, and he was gracious enough to set up a place to stay when I got out. I felt lucky to have met him.

However, as my life can never go straight as an arrow, as usual, it started to get crazy again. I met another girl while I went for a walk to the corner store. I knew the girl from jail, and she was high when I met her. We exchanged formalities, and she lured me into my one weakness; drugs. At first, I said no, when she asked me what I was looking to buy, but then I gave into my desire and figured once in a while won't do me much harm. I followed her back to her house, where she had her stash. Another guy joined us, and we smoked the whole night away. While I was enjoying this moment of epiphany, another problem was brewing for me. My pen pal had arranged for me to live at his sister's house; while the arrangement was good, I knew he would freak out if his sister saw me high on drugs. I couldn't go back to that place like this and had no choice but to move to the streets again. Again, I had done everything in my power to sabotage my life completely when it was eventually going well. I don't know why I had this repeated self-destruction pattern, but what I did know was that it was getting worse and worse by the minute. Maybe I didn't see myself living a good, sober life and subconsciously damaged all my prospects of a better life.

Anyway, moving forward, I was back to the streets again, doing what I had to do to survive and get high. I was basically back at my old routine, and even though it came with its fair share of struggles, I enjoyed every bit of it. I was back, turning to my old tricks, which required using my body to get high. Meanwhile, my pen pal had heard what I was doing, and he got mad at me for being so careless and irresponsible with my life. However, I paid no heed to his concerns and told him that he was in jail while I was not and could do whatever I wanted. I informed him in a matter of factly way that I am accustomed to living like this, and he should not be so worried about me. I knew what I was doing.

I moved into another lady's house I met while getting high, and she kindly welcomed me into her humble abode. I ran around the streets getting high without a care in the world, and well, I ended up getting pregnant again. However, this time pregnancy didn't even shock me; I was so used to getting pregnant that it didn't falter me at all. Even while I was pregnant, I was prancing around like a wild thing, stocking up my body with all kinds of drugs that I could get. If all my pregnancies had been successful, I would have been the mother of four children by now. Imagine at the age of seventeen having four children. It sounded surreal, but sadly it was true. I was abusing my body with no intention of stopping. I had learned to cash cheques and credit cards illegally, which funded my addiction, showing no signs of stopping. It was getting worse and worse, and eventually, I ended up losing my baby boy. However, that wasn't enough to stop me, and I even began to produce fraudulent cheques and tried to fool banks into giving me money. Unfortunately, it all came crumbling down when I went to cash in a bad cheque. The police and FBI were called, and I knew I was heading to jail again for the third time now. They held up a case against me for cheque frauds and materials; however, they had to drop the case because they did not have enough evidence to pursue a federal case.

I was still sentenced to two and a half years in the Ohio reformatory facility, yes, the same one I was sentenced to a while ago. I was not too fond of the place and couldn't imagine how I ended up there again. But I knew I was the one to blame yet again for all my antics. Of course, my actions and behavior brought me back. I served my time in the hole by fighting; I was venting my rage on others, and I didn't want anyone to think I was terrified because I wasn't. I determined that I needed to change my life because I did not want to spend the rest of my life in jails and prisons. But I also knew that change was inevitable until I was ready to take responsibility for my actions. As time passed, I was becoming more and more aware of my actions and wanted to improve myself. As they say, acknowledgment is the first step toward betterment, and I was ready for it, or so I thought. I hadn't thought that it was going to be a long and painful journey, and I would relapse multiple times, but if, in the end, I could reach my goal, then it would all be worth it.

When I declared that I would not return to the hole, I changed my conduct and was transported from the hole to a cottage. To pass the time, I grabbed a job and worked. My term was nearing a conclusion, and I had the option of going to Franklin County Prerelease or Northeast Prerelease, and I picked Cleveland, Ohio. I got out, but within two to three months, I was back to my old ways. I met some people at the women's shelter where I stayed and learned about all the best places to acquire crack cocaine. I stayed in the shelter trying to find a place to stay when I said I wasn't going high anymore, and I detoxed myself there with no help. I stopped going around the area. I got clean and proceeded to look for employment; I was recruited at West Park Direct, a telemarketing company, and I worked there for three months until I met someone who liked me. I eventually got an apartment and a car. We became a playhouse once he moved in with me. I was pregnant with my last child a few months down the road. A month later, I discovered that he was back on drugs, that he had my car, and that he had been gone for hours. I became concerned and began questioning him; he, of course, lied.

One night I drove him to a spot he wanted to go to. Not knowing he would buy drugs, we drove until we arrived home. Once again, he was in the bathroom with the door locked. I asked him what the hell he was doing, and he didn't say anything for a long time until I realized he was smoking crack. A few days later, I got a phone call from the lady in North Carolina, telling me she was sending my daughter back to me because she was sneaking out the windows, messing around with older guys, bringing guys in the house, etc. I was like, okay, send her to me, and I promised to be better with her this time, however that changed quickly. After nine long years of not seeing my child, I was thrilled to see her. I picked her up from the Greyhound bus station that week and got her into school as soon as possible. She was in ninth grade, and I didn't want her to miss any of her classes as the weeks passed. I began retaking drugs and received eviction letters. I'd lost my work, and my stomach had a bump, so I took the help of food stamps. I started selling them and began to owe people money.

I had to send my daughter to my mom for her not to be homeless like I was. It was clear that I was destined to be doomed, pregnant, and destitute. My kid had vanished, I had lost my job, and the baby daddy had also disappeared; he was running two women simultaneously, and one of them was pregnant. Only she had children and a home for them. I was sleeping from pillow to pillow as the baby grew. Since I was feeling ill, I had to go to the doctor, and why wouldn't I be? My situation was getting worse.

As I lay in the hospital bed, the doctor informed me that he had contacted Child Family Services because I tested positive for cocaine. They were worried about the infant. When the ladies from social services arrived at the hospital, they were pretty concerned about the kid and me, and they threatened to take him if I didn't get my act together. Oh, how I ran from those people who chased me all around Cleveland. I had to make it to a different hospital to give birth to my kid.

My baby boy was born on February 20, 2005, delivered by C-section. That's when I realized I needed to get these tubes tied. I didn't want any more kids. Three days later, they came to the hospital and took him away from me, saying, "We told you this was going to happen if you didn't do anything about your drug abuse." I cried because all of my children ended up in the state's care or with someone other than their mother. I called my mother and begged her to pick up my baby; she said, "No, Angela, this one is on you." You must organize your life, obtain your baby, and raise him. My heart was broken. Because I felt low and discouraged, I began to abuse my body more, piling up more drugs in my system.

I was hanging out in downtown Cleveland by greyhound and job and family services, doing whatever I could to avoid the agony of wanting that baby boy back. I didn't think of anyone or anything. I was numb, as if my entire universe had crumbled in front of me. I used it for around six months before I couldn't tolerate it any longer. That was all that mattered to me: I wanted my baby. On October 14, 2005, I headed down to the county jail and informed the officer that I had a warrant and wanted assistance. My judge happened to be on the bench that day. When I went to visit her, she asked, "What do you want me to do for you, Ms. Sampson?" I told her I needed help, and I would die out there if she didn't choose to help me. She said, "Okay, I'll see you later," and the bailiff led me to the holding cell. I was locked up in that cell for two hours. I began to pray while being locked up, saying, "Lord, I don't want to live like this anymore; if you take the taste out of my mouth and the yearning out of my heart, I will never do drugs again."

I slept on the bench until the judge summoned me. As I

approached the judge, she addressed me: “Ms. Sampson. I'm going to send you to Cliff Skeen CBCF in Akron until you finish your sentence. After that, I will put you on probation for one year.” It was as if a weight had been lifted off my shoulders. That was the last time I ingested any mind-altering chemical.

Chapter 10

Sober Life

The 14th of October, 2005, marked the end of my drug use. I was locked up until a bed became available. I was transferred to CBCF in December 2005. Once there, I began to examine my life honestly and realized that I did not want to go down that road again. As a result, I needed to do whatever it took to stay sober. I was able to see my baby because I followed all of the DCFS personnel's instructions. Those three months seemed endless, but I did what I had to do for him. He required the assistance of his mother. He was a part of me just as much as I was a part of him.

I completed phase one of the intake processes and then began my treatment process, attending the group every day from 9 a.m. to 12 p.m., then lunch, and then back to the group from 1 p.m. to 4 p.m. for 60 days. After finishing treatment, I was free to look for work; I acquired a position through a temp agency and saved money. Furthermore, I could go on the pass for the weekend and stay with a buddy. He was a good person, but I didn't want to be in a relationship, so it was tough for me to come home for the weekend; I was attending meetings every weekend.

I introduced myself to this lady and told her about my situation; she was a homegroup member I was attending. She invited me to stay with her, which I accepted because I liked her. After that, everything fell into place; I was able to see my child more frequently now that I had a location for him to visit. I had been successfully discharged from treatment, so I boarded the bus from Akron to Cleveland, where she met me and brought me to her home. I was attending meetings and doing everything I could to maintain my sobriety. Finally, I met a sponsor, who walked me through the 12 steps in a single day. I wasn't sure if I was going to make it.

However, I continued to pray and express my fears and sentiments. Finally, my coworkers persuaded me to continue with my treatment. As a result, I enrolled in Matt Talbott Inn IOP. I had 12 weeks of treatment left, and I was disappointed at first, but my workers assured me that they would reunite me with my child once I finished. I ended up booking a hotel at Cleveland's Scarborough House on the city's west side. I went to a meeting across the street at a church. I was required to attend three AA meetings every week as part of the house rules.

I arrived at the meeting, walked in, placed my paper on the table, and sat in front. I spotted this nice-looking man staring at me, but I tried not to act on my thoughts. As the session came to a close, he handed me my paper and added, "Use that phone number," to which I grinned. My thoughts arose, "He's a jerk. Fine." I reasoned I needed him in my life.

He came up behind me with this big ass tub, slapping me in the ass as I climbed up the steps to the door. I turned around and locked my gaze on him. Oh, dang! He was overjoyed. We were outside conversing when he said to me, "I'm married but unhappy." Damn, there they come again. When I fell at this time, I told myself, "OK, I'll contact you later." So I went back to the sober house and called him, just as I had promised. We talked every day, and when he came to pick me up one night, we went to the lake and talked about everything. He'd become a friend of mine. He'd tell me about his upbringing and marriage. He'd also say he didn't want to injure anyone, which was understandable. I was thinking in my thoughts, forget it, I want him, and I'm going to get him no matter what.

Things quickly became serious between us, and we began spending time together in hotels. Everything was going well. I lived in a house with three other females, all of whom were quite nice to me. I went to Geauga Lake with one of the females, and we became great friends, but she had money, was a nurse, and couldn't drive her car without blowing into the tube because she had too many DUIs.

Again I was tempted when I saw her laptop and wanted one for myself as well. Anyway, I grabbed her credit card from her wallet and used it to buy a laptop for myself. Of course, accusations were brought against me, and I was compelled to leave the premises. I called that special friend and told him what was going on, telling him I was on probation, and he was relieved. The next day, I had to see my probation officer, and when I told him what had happened, he promptly locked me up. I'd been in the county jail for three days when a special friend visited me one day before my release.

I was given eight months to fulfill my probation in 2006. I was still sober when I returned to prison. Things seemed bizarre, and I pondered how I got up like this again. My reasoning was still skewed, but I figured I could get away with it. I was in Marysville for four months and didn't have to worry about anything because my excellent lover cared for everything. He would send me money once a week. And cards that expressed everything there was to say. So I began my term at Marysville, where I glanced out the window before being transferred to Northeast Pre-release to finish it.

I used to look out the window every day, hoping to see him ride by because he knew I was in pre-release. I spent as much time as I could on the phone with him. I visited my little boy whenever I was down because his foster parents had taken him to see me.

That was the case till I escaped. He was always there for me, no matter what. I went to the counselor, and she helped me get into a phase one program. I called my unique buddy and told him I needed some clothes to return home in, and he went out of his way to help me.

He was there to pick me up when the time arrived for me to be released. We went to the hotel and had a good time. He drove me to phase one, where I was staying, and I've seen him almost every day since. I even saw his daughter once, and she was the sweetest little child I'd ever seen, and I think she also liked me. I lived in a house with six other women, and we got along great. I continued to pay visits to my son on occasion.

"Let's get your baby home to you," my social worker remarked one day when she came to visit me. I needed to get him into a transitional housing facility, so I set to work. I was interviewed for transitional housing and waited at phase one until a bed became available. It wasn't just a bed, though; it was a tiny apartment. I moved into transitional housing. At Bryant and Stratton College, I enrolled in a medical assistant program. I had to return to court for my son or recover possession, which was a time-consuming process. I had the impression that this guy's parents were not attempting to return my son to me, and I fought them tooth and nail because he did not belong to them, he belonged to me, and I was free, and I wanted my son back. My social workers fought for me in court because they wanted my son to be with me. Finally, I regained custody of my kid, who was brought to me at a transitional housing facility. I had to change rooms since the one I was in was too small for both of us. Even though he was only two years old, having a baby seemed unusual. I loved every minute of it.

I took him to school and dropped him off at childcare every day. I drove him home after picking him up. That remarkable man of mine came over one day and assembled a toddler bed for my son so he could sleep. It was humorous because he could get in and put the bed together even though men were not permitted on the grounds. "There's your daddy," I told the baby when he came to see me one day. My special friend arrived with a car seat, a cap, and glasses for his youngster the next day. Even though he claims I placed a baby on his lap, he was his son; the moral of the story is that he had all girls and no boy, so I gave him one.

Other than this, I was working hard to establish a career for which I needed an education. Every day, I went to school, telling myself that it was time to obtain a job or go to school. I chose to go to school since I was receiving financial aid to help pay my rent. I also applied for food stamps so we could eat. Going to school was difficult because my classrooms were in the same neighborhood where I used to get high. But I persisted in praying and discussing it with my sponsor. I attended meetings three times per week, and a close buddy made sure that I heard some of his sessions. Life was starting to get better. I wanted to work, but no one was interested in hiring me because of my lengthy criminal record and probation. This was getting on my nerves. Finally, my caseworkers persuaded me to continue treatment. Then, I went to school, which was extremely frustrating because I received all of them through the medical aid program to find out that I had to interview for training and no one would touch me because of my background, so I ended up changing degrees to criminal justice. Finally, my associate's degree was completed, which I found enjoyable. I learned about a transitory family housing program that would place you in a house if you passed the interview. I did, and we were able to move out of temporary accommodation and into our own home. It wasn't the most suitable location on the planet, but it sufficed for the time being. Later, I ended up moving into the Scarborough house.

On and off, my special friend came to visit me whenever it was possible for him. One day his wife had a shattered ankle and was in the hospital, and he came to spend the night with me. He contacted me on his way to work that morning and said, "Aj, whatever you do, don't come outside." "I'll tell you later," he answered when I asked him why. To cut a long story short, at night, the house was infested with spiders. So he went out and bought some spray that killed them, and the following week I moved into a townhouse via a transitional family program. My specific friend left for Christmas with his family a few months later; I missed him, but he managed to phone me daily. When he got back, he came to see me and gave me a gift, a handheld camcorder, and some toys for Cj. His wife was not good to him, and my special friend contacted me once to say he needed a place to stay since his daughter had told his wife about me, and she had evicted him. So I told him he could stay here if he wanted. I had grown to love him at this point and to be honest, and I had loved him since the beginning. So he moved in, and he was no longer my special friend; he had become my man, and I had him all to myself.

At first, we had a fantastic relationship, but we had to relocate because the family transition had shifted to Westside Catholic. They hauled in all of the units and distributed Section 8 coupons. So we found a house on Cleveland's west side and relocated. I didn't know how to treat a man correctly because of all the trauma I had with men, and he noticed it daily. I couldn't even apologize for inflicting anguish on this man.

We had a heated argument one day. When I go home the next day, he has a U-Haul, and his wife is at my house assisting him with his relocation back home. I lost my mind. I felt as if I had an out-of-body experience. I fought up the wife, threw stuff around, swiped his credit card jar, and paid some bills because I was hurt, which isn't an excuse because my attitude caused everything to happen. Then, I drove to their house on the other side of town and destroyed his new truck's mirror. "I'll show you who to fool with," I yelled, enraged. I just cried like a baby after it all happened, wondering what I had done to deserve this.

For about two weeks, everything was calm until I went to school as usual and received a call from him stating he missed me and wanted to see me. He stated that he was still dissatisfied. We had another argument while I was at work, so I left and told myself I was going to Walmart, where I knew he would be, but I did not expect to see him with his wife again, especially after he told me nothing had changed between them.

I acted irrationally once more. I jumped on him in the Walmart parking lot and ended up in jail for the weekend. I phoned him while I was there, and he said he didn't press charges because he loved me and knew I was acting out of rage. I didn't bother him at all when I got home on Sunday. I convinced myself that it was over and that I couldn't bother him anymore. When he contacted me two weeks later to say he wanted to meet with me, I said, "Come on through." We were back in business after he arrived. I had a soft spot in my heart for this man. To me, he was like a best friend.

I moved to West 130th in 2009, and since then, I have been sober for six years. After graduating from college, I decided to enhance my education by enrolling at Cleveland State University to pursue a double major in Criminology and Sociology.

When I finished in 2012, I was tired of playing mind games with him, so I brought another man into the house with me. It was either shit or got off the pot to show that I was no longer interested in playing with him. But I didn't desire that man deep down, and I moved in because it wasn't in my heart. I couldn't take my eyes off the man I adored. We kept chatting on and off, and he'd even come to see me; I was so good that I'd tell the other man to go because my baby's father was coming over, and I didn't want him to see you here. That went on for a whole year until I dared to talk it out with the one I truly wanted to be with. Finally, things were starting to look hopeful.

I hold a master's degree in addiction therapy, a master's degree in social work, and a Ph.D. in psychology. I'm an Independent Chemical Dependency Counselor with a license. I own and run a rehab facility for adult men who have mental illnesses and substance misuse. My husband, three children, and three grandchildren make my life complete. I'm grateful to God for everyone in my life. I'm approaching 16 years of sobriety, and my life couldn't have been better. I couldn't believe I'd accomplished it.

I fear to think what would have occurred if I hadn't taken this extreme step to transform my life. Life would be very different right now, and not in a good way. My life would have been brief, if not horrible, and I have no idea what would have happened to my children. They'd probably be bounced around from foster care until they became independent and developed bad habits, just like their mother.

I will be eternally grateful for everyone's assistance and support; I could not have done this without it. I wouldn't have been as successful if the judge hadn't assisted me in changing my life, as that was a critical step on the road to recovery. That day, she showed me kindness, for which I will always be grateful.

Made in the USA
Coppell, TX
11 February 2022